MW01278568

DAD
‿

MARGARET LANNAMANN

DESIGNED BY DIANE HOBBING

ARIEL BOOKS

**Andrews McMeel
Publishing**

Kansas City

ISBN: 0-7407-3366-4
Library of Congress Catalog Card Number: 2002111884

DAD

INTRODUCTION

Our DADS are teachers, nurturers, and protectors. They play with us, laugh with us, and best of all, they love us unconditionally.

When we need someone to hold us tight and keep us safe, they're always there. When we need someone to inspire and encourage us, they cheer us on. When we need someone to brighten our day, they tell us jokes and make us smile.

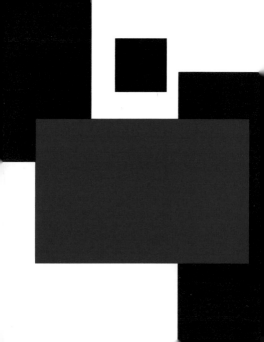

They are our constant support, the framework of our lives.

This book is a tribute to all the DADS everywhere whose love helps make us who we are.

What's the most special thing about being a father?

DAD

EVERYTHING.

—Viggo Mortensen

I took a first look at my son, and it was instantaneous, unconditional love. It was wild.

—Kevin Sorbo

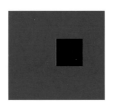

DAD

As a parent, you are your child's safe harbor. You're the island in the middle of the ocean they call home.

—Phillip McGraw

Watching
your child run into
your outstretched
arms is one of the
most wonderful
sights in the world.

The thing I enjoy most about being a D_AD is being a kid again, with him. It's the little things, everyday moments we spend together, like sitting and having breakfast, the ride to school, hanging out.

—Dennis Quaid

It's the most wonderful way to live, being a father. It balances out the lunacy of acting. Parenthood keeps you young, in tune with life and in tune with yourself.

—Pierce Brosnan

Tucking a child in at **night** is the perfect ending to any day.

When you're drawing up your first list of life's miracles, you might place near the top the first moment your baby smiles at you.

—Bob Greene

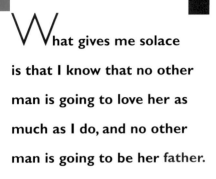

What gives me solace is that I know that no other man is going to love her as much as I do, and no other man is going to be her father.

—Damian Millea

19

But when you come home at night with only the shat-tered pieces of your hopes and dreams, he can mend them like new with two magic words—"Hi, ᗡA⊡ !"

—Alan Beck

ᗡA⊡

When dealing with children, it's nice to be the font of all knowledge, but with children, **listening** can be more important than talking.

The toughest job in the world isn't being president. It's being a parent.

—Bill Clinton

As a teenager, I rebelled and wanted to break out of the confines of my strict upbringing. But now . . . I'm becoming more like my father.

—Denzel Washington

23

Keep in mind that your son's or daughter's **dreams** may be different from your own.

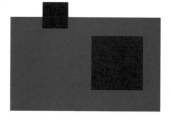

DAD

I talk and talk and talk, and I haven't taught people in fifty years what my father taught by example in one week.

—Mario Cuomo

Parents are not quite interested in justice. They are interested in quiet.

—Bill Cosby

When in doubt,
take pictures.

Life affords no greater responsibility, no greater privilege, than the raising of the next generation.

—C. Everett Koop

Success is a man whose children love him and have made him proud of them.

—David Brown

Job description for dads:

Must be **loving, strong,** and **good at jokes.** Skills in **ball throwing, hugging,** and **tickling** a plus. Must expect long hours; pay is all the **love** you can hold.

Other things may change us, but we start and end with the family.

—Anthony Brandt

I don't give my children advice unless they ask.

—Rip Torn

DAD

Never underestimate the power of a hug and a quick **"I love you,"** even when the object of your affection is squirming to run out the door.

Children are the living messages we send to a time we will not see.

—Neil Postman

I still—to a very great measure—want to impress my father.

—Peter Jennings

Ten best
things about
being a dad:

hugs, dancing together around the kitchen, listening to endless "knock-knock" jokes, the feel of a small hand in yours, reading together, walks through piles of autumn leaves, sticky kisses, watching the excited anticipation of holidays, teaching the skill of bike riding, saying "I love you" and meaning it with every fiber of your being.

37

The greatest happiness I've ever had in my life comes from my daughter. Watching her grow. Talking to her.

—Mort Zuckerman

Nothing I've ever done has given me more joys and rewards than being a father to my five.

—Bill Cosby

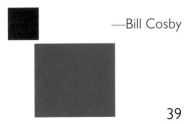

I want my kids to see the world with an open mind and an open heart. To stand up for themselves and not fall for

DAD

anything. To try to experience as much as they can now, so they have that to draw from as they get older.

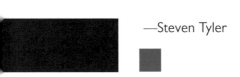

—Steven Tyler

Once you're a
father, you're a father

F o r e

D_AD

ver.

43

Using television as a babysitter can be bad for kids, but watching television *with* your kids can create a p o s i t i v e, bonding experience.

DAD

I'm a musician, a pianist, a guy from Long Island. A father, most importantly of all.

—Billy Joel

Be there. Be there for your kids. Think of it this way: If life were a Hollywood film, DAD wouldn't be the star. He wouldn't be the director. He wouldn't be a stuntman. He'd be the best supporting actor. It's the role of a lifetime.

—David Shribman

The idea of celebrating
Father's Day

began in 1909 when Sonora Smart Dodd looked for a way to honor her father. Today we celebrate Father's Day on the third Sunday in June, a date close to Sonora's father's birthday, which was June 19.

DAD

You know your children are growing up when they start asking questions that have answers.

—John J. Plomp

Anyone can have a child. It's a different thing entirely to be a

father.

DAD

A father is a man who expects his son to be as good a man as he meant to be.

—Frank A. Clark

Your children need your
presence more than your
presents.

—Jesse Jackson

DAD

Train up a child in the way
he should go—and walk there
yourself once in a while.

—Josh Billings

The best thing you can give your children is the gift of yourself.

DAD

Children . . . they string our joys, like jewels bright, upon the thread of years.

—Edward A. Guest

Give the **gift** of a skill:
Teach your child to build a
bookshelf, change a tire, or
write a résumé.

DAD

Nothing is so potent as the silent influence of a good example.

—James Kent

Some favorite films about fathers: **Kramer vs. Kramer** with Dustin Hoffman and Meryl Streep, **Father's Day** with Robin Williams and Billy Crystal, **Father of the Bride** with Steve Martin and Kimberly Williams, **Mrs. Doubtfire** with Robin Williams, **Nothing in Common** with Tom Hanks, **Mr. Mom** with Michael

DAD

Keaton, **My Girl** with Dan Akroyd and Anna Chlumsky, and **Three Men and a Baby** with Tom Selleck, Steve Guttenberg, and Ted Danson.

If your teenager doesn't act as if you're dumb and a real **embarrassment** at times, you may not be doing your job right.

DAD

Before I got married I had six theories about bringing up children; now I have six children and no theories.

—John Wilmot

A father is

a pillar of strength,
a problem solver, a
tower of wisdom,
a source of love, and
the only one who
knows how to fix the
kitchen sink when it
gets clogged up.

I could now afford all the things I never had as a kid, if I didn't have kids.

—Robert Orben

It's extraordinary to me that my son would listen to and have faith in whatever wisdom I can offer.

—Tom Hanks

DAD

Plant a tree each time a child or grandchild is born.

It doesn't make any difference how much money a father earns, his name is always D𝐀D-Can-I . . .

—Bill Cosby

When things get tough, you can always comfort yourself by saying, "It's just a phase."

Fatherhood **is the**

greatest opportunity in the

world—to have children

and watch them grow at

various stages of life.

—Bill Bell

DAD

Often the deepest relation-
ships can be developed during
the simplest activities.

—Gary Smalley

The only rock I know that stays steady, the only institution I know that works, is the

family.

—Lee Iacocca

DAD

I don't mind looking into the mirror and seeing my father.

—Michael Douglas

A good rule to follow
is to be sure that each time
you criticize your child, you
praise that same child
twice.

DAD

According to statistics from AT&T, daughters call their fathers more than twice as often as sons do, children call their fathers more often than fathers call their children, and the number of men and women calling their fathers on Father's Day are more or less equal.

Parents can plant magic in a child's mind through certain words spoken with some thrilling quality of voice, some uplift of the heart and spirit.

—Robert MacNeil

DAD

The only way we can ever teach a child to say "I'm sorry" is for him to hear it from our lips first.

—Kevin Leman

"I'm sorry"

Why is it that our kids are totally unable to work the vacuum cleaner or the lawnmower, but they have **no trouble** at all learning to drive the car?

DAD

A father
is a coach
on life.

One of the greatest **pleasures** can be reading aloud to a son or daughter. As your child grows older, you can continue to share the wonder of books by each **reading** the same story and talking about it afterward.

DAD

Raising kids is part joy and part guerrilla warfare.

—Ed Asner

In memory of my

D_AD

George Stevenson

Book design and composition
by Diane Hobbing of
Snap-Haus Graphics
in Dumont, NJ

DAD